A SPRINKLE OF NUTMEG

Phyl Fry

A SPRINKLE OF NUTMEG

LETTERS TO CHRISTOPHER FRY 1943–45

with a foreword by Christopher Fry

London
ENITHARMON PRESS
1992

First published in 1992
by the Enitharmon Press
36 St George's Avenue
London N7 0HD

Distributed in Europe
by Password (Books) Ltd.
23 New Mount Street
Manchester M4 4DE

Distributed in the USA
by Dufour Editions Inc.
PO Box 449, Chester Springs
Pennsylvania 19425

ISBN 1 870612 58 2 (paperback)
ISBN 1 870612 63 9 (hardback)

The paperback edition numbers 2000 copies;
the cloth edition is limited to 50 copies, signed and
numbered by Christopher Fry.

The proceeds from *A Sprinkle of Nutmeg*
will be donated to
The Child Growth Foundation, Charity Registered No. 274325

The recreation on page 34 of Christopher Fry's Valentine card
is by Julian Bell, as is the drawing on page 63.

Set in 10½pt Bembo by Bryan Williamson, Darwen
and printed in Great Britain
by
Antony Rowe Ltd, Chippenham, Wiltshire

And oft the pangs of absence to remove
By letters, soft interpreters of love

Matthew Prior

FOREWORD

From December 1940 until September 1944 Phyl and I were in different parts of England, except for the days when I was on leave – Phyl for a time in the Welsh mountains helping to look after children evacuated from the cities – while I was fire-watching on the Liverpool Docks, or in London or in Derby, according to the job in hand. In August 1942 Phyl took a job as domestic-help at a little school for under-eight-year-olds (Miss Thomson, Principal) at Fulbrook, a mile outside Burford in the Cotswolds. The good purpose of this was that Phyl could add to the small army allowance and yet be with Tam while he had some schooling. He was five years old when they went there.

For the next two years Phyl's letters came from Cotter's Bow, or, on her day off, from The Buildings, two stone cottages huddled together face to face on a wide hill above Shipton-under-Wychwood, the front windows no further apart than would give bare room for a farm tractor to drive between them. One was lived in by the carter and his wife, Mr and Mrs Stoter, whose married son Norris, or Norrie, lived farther down the hill. The other had once housed the shepherd; but lately the farmer, Mr Holloway, known as Mister, had been using it for storing sacks of corn. He was a widower living with his sister, called 'Aunty' by all of us. Phyl and I had been homeless since the sale of the cottage we once rented in the village. When I was on leave we had nowhere of our own to go to, until kind Mister gave the shepherd's cottage a lick of whitewash and let it to us for three shillings a week. Adjoining the cottage was a wash-house, with one tap and a copper for heating water, which we shared with the Stoters. Round the corner was a privy containing a bucket. The Buildings were four miles from Cotter's Bow. In the earliest of these extracts from her letters Phyl describes the bicycle ride to Shipton and the ride 'home' as she calls it, though it was Cotter's Bow she was returning to. The letters from the first year at the school have, alas, disappeared, so Mrs Crook the cook, who lived with her farmer husband across the road, and Doris a housemaid, and Spy, Mrs Crook's dog, come to us unintroduced, along with the two Marys on the staff, and Miss Thomson's mother, and another Miss Thomson who taught dancing, and, among the pupils, the artists Edward and Charlotte

Bawden's daughter Joanna. Their son Richard was there, too, and the two sons of a fellow artist Eric Ravilious, though they don't come into the book. And there were the Lovell brothers, and Gavin Wetton, and Pat (or Tricia) Scott, a seventeen-year-old assistant to the matron, and her little sister Julia who was given cottage-room at The Buildings during the summer holidays.

Down in the valley at Shipton lived Ella Hewlett, widowed sister-in-law of the novelist Maurice Hewlett, and her sister Margie; and in the other direction, at Burford, were the Boulters. Mrs Boulter taught music at Cotter's Bow; Ben Boulter was a retired headmaster. Why Phyl decided to have German lessons with him I'm not sure, though when she heard that Robert Gittings and his wife had gone for a five mile walk talking Italian all the way she wrote 'a damping setback for me when I considered that the only slightly foreign thing I could say to you in five miles was Ya Vas Loublou.'

In March 1944 something happened which altogether changed our prospects, which gave us breathing space when the War ended, so that I could finish one play and write *A Phoenix Too Frequent.* I sent a letter to Phyl giving her the news on 'March 16 at a guess', though I think it was more likely to have been the 18th, since Phyl's happy reply was dated March 21. I was working then in the Army Post-office, sometimes by day, sometimes on night-shift:

Toc H Canteen
Nottingham

March 16 at a guess 1944

...The most interesting part of this letter comes last: I'll keep you in delicious suspense...Slinging mailbags all day. Isn't it nice that a stinking parcel when opened should turn out to be Fish and Chips, sent out on an eight weeks' journey (at least) with a message to say "Knowing how you love fish and chips", etc...Last night one of the packages came undone while the girls were sorting, and in it was a photograph of a middle-aged woman – I wish I could make you see it: by a cheap studio photographer: a most dear and motherly person, making a grimace: an enormous bosom hanging almost to her knees: rather bandy in the legs; and on the back was written: To my darling son I am sorry but the photo did not come out as well as I had hoped it would have. I had tryed a smile but it did not work nise. I will smile better when I see you home please God. Love from Mum. – Perhaps that's an easy lump in the throat, but it got it from me. – But you probably can't take any interest in all this because you're impatient to hear the news. It's on the other side of the page.

We are temporarily people of private means, dearest heart. Jack is letting us have two hundred pounds a year, free of tax, for seven years.

Phyl, in her reply, had difficulty in taking it in: 'Perhaps if you send me a small carefree cheque to buy a new frock to wear to Nottingham, or a Bristol bowl to wear on my mantelpiece, it will be brought home to me.'

When six of the years were up *The Lady's not for Burning* had run its course in London, *Venus Observed* had just opened at the St James's, and the time of almost daily letter-writing was a part of history.

C.F.

Last night I started on the monumental Everestian job of sorting out our letters, and yesterday I went to Mr Miles and ordered an Oak Box to hold the letters we write to each other for the rest of our lives because with careful packing the Bible-box should see us through the war. I told him nearly as large as a tuck-box, and oak and to make it so that it would last 300 years. He warmed to the suggestion that he should carve the date on it . . . It will be several months making. I'm putting them in large envelopes in years: Christopher Fry to Phyllis Fry 1942; all very efficient, but it takes so long because I have to read them all . . . All the love that has gone into these letters for 3 years should keep us warm and strong all the rest of our lives.

January 13, 1944

June 2, 1943
Flaming Wet

... Yesterday we had a new boy; I spent a long time telling Tam how delicate he was and how he'd spent months in bed and how his hands wouldn't work properly and how nice it would be if Tam were extra kind to him because he'd be a bit shy and strange when lo and behold – he turns out to have shot up in his bed to about five feet high at 6 years and to look like some underground weed with hysterical strength; he never stops talking and he bangs and pinches everyone he meets; he's probably kicked Tam downstairs twice by now, which serves me right for interfering...

Yesterday Tuesday was my Sunday out, and never did the tempest so pour and rage; going over the hill the rain swept at my back like a blast from a hose pipe. There was a lovely time when the road was washing and swishing like a river and the tall green and purple grasses at the sides of the road were bent and poured all one way by the wind so that it seemed as if I sailed down a river with a strong tide... There never was air so washed and shining as the air on our hill when the rain was over, it was cleaner than a whistle and brighter than a new peeled stick and the hedges smoked with scent of roses.

Cotter's Bow
August 10, 1943

. . . General Browne has been here for the weekend to keep Mrs T(homson) company . . . They chirped gently together from morning till night and when I went into the room I caught a waft of: . . . "No, my dear, it must have been *well* before '78, because I remember Fred and I were both subalterns . . . " – "Now I remember him well, he had the same name as that Scotch doctor who set up the only military hospital when we were out there for the Boxer Rising . . . what was it?" Such a darling faded trembly pink old bore, Joe is – and he's probably responsible for the deaths of thousands of men.

The Cottage
October 10, 1943

This is the cottage with the lamp lit and Tuesday my Sunday out. Just now I should be in Burford listening to Dr Palimpsest but by the time I'd had a long talk from Miss Bowerman about Unity Mitford and the iniquitous chiropodist and then a long welcome talk and thank you to Mrs Stoter up here who'd lit my fire and laid out 4 mouse bodies for me to see – 5 if you count the one the cat ate, it was getting on for 4.30 and time to think of getting back to Burford for the lecture. So I didn't think of it, but had tea with toast and crapple jelly left by Mary Bawden, and arranged a large pile of white chrysanthemums given by Mrs Stoter. The room looks now as if 2 large white swans had alighted in it and gone to roost one on top of the tallboy and one in the window... Yesterday morning I made a neat jingling poem before I woke, but though I dived back into my sleep, the only line I could fish up was:

"And give the dawn a rusty break."

Very funny if my unconscious turns out to be Ella Wheeler Wilcox or Saml. Smiles.

October 15, 1943

My face is sore from the lashings of cow tails: I felt I should go out and do some milking this afternoon; it's 16 years since I've milked, and the cow resented it and whipped her tail across my face and told the cow next to her to do the same with her tail, and then she trod her hoof on my best suede shoe which I shouldn't have worn for milking. I worked hard for about a quart of milk, but by tomorrow I shall have remembered the rhythm.

October 16, 1943

In this very hand that salutes you is a new fountain pen! Got simply for the asking in Shipton Post Office on this my Friday out. I asked Mrs Wiggins if I could go down on her list when she had a fountain pen in her shop, and as casual as all get out she said she'd just got a large consignment in! Nothing like that has ever happened before to me and now I'm writing you a flowing letter from my bed with a warm hot water bottle on my stomach and Mary Charles has just brought up a handsome hot drink of Lime juice cordial for me. And the pen was only 4/3 all told. So with that and *Woman and Beauty* and 24 sheets of beautiful green wrapping paper for 1/- I rode back to the cottage through a sunset whose sun had come through the mist for the first time today. And the sun made a thick deep yellow light on the underside of everything so that looking down Shipton Court yellow elm avenue was like looking through a bright pot of Golden Shred marmalade, and all the horses' bellies were luminous... Then with the last dying light I turned my kitchen out – all the cupboard contents were to be vice-versa except that the dark came and I couldn't see which I was turning out of one place and which I was putting back in another. Then it was too dark to do anything except draw the curtains and light the lamp and candles and boil an egg with 2 bits of toast and three cups of coffee and read. I *did* read *Woman and Beauty* but I thought noble thoughts to make up for it while I was cycling home... I swam over the top of the hill like a fish through moonstone mist lit with a grey candle of moon – and this is my lovely, lovely bed.

I'm getting very fond of our Doris: she has a most endearing way of arranging the face flannels when she cleans the Blue bathroom. There's a broad tiled window sill, and the flannels have usually been folded and draped over the edge in a hygienic straight line, but Doris has fantasticated the whole process and folds each flannel like a table napkin into whorls and long rolls and triangles and then makes a sort of formal patterned flower border with them on the sill and each day the pattern is different. Today, to my surprise, the flannels were folded and twisted to say T A M; I daren't tell him because he'll rush round the place telling everyone, which will lead to hard feelings; maybe she's going to sculpt the name of every boy in the bathroom and started with the easiest.

... This dinner time Mrs Crook was disposing of a big ham bone and we naturally said: Give it to Spy. She said No; if you givs it to Spy it will make him sick, ham bones always do make a dog sick, but if you throw it over the wall and Spy happens to find it, he won't be ill. For ninstance (her favourite word) if I has a cutting giv to me out of the garden I can't make um grow, but if I steals um, he'll thrive.

And I had a lovely dream this morning which I must tell you because it makes such a lovely picture, in contrast to my usual dreams which are squalid to say the least. I was with you in a pew in a village church; there was a bowl of flowers in our pew and I was twisting a branch of a very unknown very lovely blue flower. I looked up to the chancel end which was like an alcove with pillars and the ceiling painted like an Italian church, all very light and full of sunshine and colour, and at the side was a wonderful group of real people arranged like a Gainsborough period family group with a stout flowing mother with high wig in the middle and many sons and daughters around her. Then the stout flowing mother stood up and said to the Churchful: We won't wait for him any longer, and she strode up to the altar but stood behind it as if it were a counter. We all stood up, and the service was about to begin among the sun and flowers when an elderly man came through the open church door; he was tall and thin and frail and wore an aristocratic chalk stripe blue suit and carried a bowler hat and was obviously just down from London. He put down a brief case, said: Very sorry everyone, trains very late, and walked up to the altar where his wife seemed to disappear and he seemed to officiate in a full bottomed wig. But the lovely thing was that at this moment a disembodied cherub's head with bright coloured wings floated around the church, like a Perugino cherub, and you said to me in a whisper pointing to it: Look, Guthrie doesn't seem to have been the youngest after all.

My milking's been put a stop to by Miss Thomson, who didn't come to me and say I might injure an expensive cow, which I should have sympathised with, but went to Mr Crook and told him she wouldn't have me learning to milk on *her* cows, and so on in the tone she keeps for the lower orders.

October 20, 1943

. . . If you think that speaking to Miss T about her cow removes any misunderstanding – well, you don't know Miss T and the workings of her mind. She is the final masterpiece of inwound elision and obliquity and there is no directness in her; to start with she never listens to what is said. I chose my moment well – usually one can only speak to her just outside the lavatory door when one of us is wanting to go in, or in the split second before the bell rings for me to serve a meal. Also I slightly rehearsed myself so that I should get first things first; then I told her that I was a little cross because she had spoken to Crook and not to me about milking her cow, but I quite understood and my milking would be in abeyance. Before I got the first three words out of my mouth she flowed a tirade at me about how valuable her cows were and how much she'd just paid in vet's bills for some damage our land girl might have done to their teats. After 10 minutes I just gave up, and since then she has twice run after me with the same vet's bill and an air of aggrieved justification . . . Last night we went to Simon's Close in howling gales to hear Dr Lampert on the first part of Soviet Russia.

October 27, 1943

. . . I *was* so cross today – and *am*: Dr Neill Crystal who is they say so famous, was to give his lecture here today to the children on insects and with slides, and Miss T had all the children excited about a *Treat*. Then she suddenly announced that it was only for the children over seven. I thought it was very hard on the others, because there's no harm in showing children things that are too difficult for them, and as they all sit still for an hour in church there's no reason why they shouldn't have sat still looking at lantern slides. And when I think that for Tam's age they only do two hours' work a day and spend the rest puddling in that damnable sand pit, it did seem to me that when an intelligent outside influence was available all the children should be able to make what they could of it. But it was no use, and I'm still cross . . . And it was evidently an extremely good lecture . . . I've just been to call Tam for his ¼ to 6 but he doesn't think he can come because he's out on the end of a branch of one of our highest trees. It doesn't look as if he can get down by bed time.

October 30, 1943

Yesterday was my Friday and a buxom day out; I split my sides to get up to the cottage quickly with a large fence of autumn boughs and pinkish reddish chrysanthemums making a windbreak in my bicycle basket, and I cleaned and warmed and polished against Mary Gardiner and Charlotte Bawden coming up for their week end. I find the mice are beyond a joke – in the side room they've eaten quite half a copy of *Horizon* and intend making their way down all the pile – in the kitchen they've eaten two sheets of cupboard paper I put on two shelves to impress the guests, and when I opened the cupboard under the stairs the wet brown stench was indescribable; next Friday I must have everything out and a cat in. I think I've lived and let live long enough, don't you? Then with a final scrabble I arranged in the small window looking out on the fowl yard the copper bowl full of copper leaves and rose chrysanthemums and orange marigolds: I thought it looked wonderful, but Mrs Bawden being an artist will probably throw up. Then I had a cup of tea with Mary who'd just come up, and cycled down the village before Charlotte arrived.

I had supper with Ella and Margie and Miss Rutherford who works at the London Library and was decently swathed in a black afternoon dress and paisley shawl and makes continual munching noises between her chin and false teeth, even when she isn't eating. But she's nice, and extremely intelligent, in a vague way and has seen all the plays and knows what's wrong with everything. We had a most sumptuous supper of mushrooms on toast and a sort of tomato charlotte and preserved pears with lovely lovely cloves (never embalm me – just lay me aside with a few cloves and a sprinkle of nutmeg) then I cycled home in warm dark.

November 2, 1943

. . . This was the Tuesday night we should have gone to [a lecture on] Russia, but it was a damping melancholy night with a difficult supper of rice and one tin of Grade 3 Salmon between 9 people; I couldn't trust its elasticity in the hands of anyone else, so I didn't go. And I've come early to bed because I'm worn out by upsetting a complete saucepan full of rice over the 4 burner oil stove – sticky white maggots of rice persisted in every nook and cranny and crevice and pipe of the oil stove, and there was no end to them. I scooped up as much as possible and sent it in to be eaten; I was too exhausted to go into supper myself so I don't know how many people were sickened with paraffin rice.

. . . On Saturday afternoon Mary Charles went to tea with Dr Christie (naturalist and great friend of Nora Nicholson) who gave her the most exquisite and macabre green and silver creaking beetle. It was sent to him by a lumber man at the docks who forgot to enclose a bit of its natal raw mahogany and having tried splinters of piano which the insect rejects, there's nothing to do but let it die in its 4 square tobacco tin.

November 17, 1943

This was a pleasant birthday; I told Tam last night so that I should have *one* greeting this morning and it was very successful: Gavin Wetton aged seven threw his arms round my neck and kissed me, smashing 3 plates I held in my hand so that I had to buy 3 plates for Cotter's Bow; then Tam gave me a dog-eared chewed up Farm Book, saying This is for you, Mummy, I don't want it; also a simply lovely key to a mechanical toy, if I had a mechanical toy, also a pack of cards that I had to give back because they belonged to Joanna Bawden...

The Stoters are a pretty sight by lamplight: she, all plump and wheezy with her knitting, and carter making his rag rugs and siffling through his black falling moustache. He's going to make me a rag rug on sacking next winter – perhaps we can incorporate your khaki trousers by then. It would be nice to trample on them for the rest of our lives.

December 9, 1943

. . . The real news of course is that the (Oswald) Mosleys with retinue and 5 cars, so they say, have taken The Shaven Crown, lock stock and beer barrels, and Shipton is full of reporters and resentment, and Mrs Thomson is about to write to the MEMBER about it. I'm due to Ella's for supper tomorrow night, the first time I've been out since you went, but I don't think I can make the effort necessary to garner the gossip.

December 13, 1943

. . . We have a little girl here called Diana Parker-Jervis who is the loveliest creature I've ever seen: transparently fair of face with thin eyebrows that point upwards at the end, and hair like pale canary's feathers. She's so delicate that she spends most of her time in bed with a cold, but even with a pink nose and blurred eyes she's exquisite.

January 15, 1944

You must really pull yourself together and start to put 1944 on top of letters, or I shall find your Biography middling muddling... What a day yesterday was – complete and perfect June from the knees up and Flanders winter 1917 from the knees down. I had to go to Burford for Hair at 5 pm so Tam went to Holloways and I started off with my bicycle making horrid janglings. I decided I needed oil but was too lazy to go back and get it. Along the top road the jangling worsened and homely peasant women and children gazed in amazement. I decided I must buy *more* oil as I thought of all the little balls and bearings retching together in rust. But Hollises hadn't got any, though after much pleading the man went out to his workshop and brought his own oil can to my bicycle outside the shop. He looked at the wheel and said "My God, miss, you've had a close shave!" And sure enough, both nuts that held the wheel into the fork were loosened to their last thread and he said that in 5 minutes the front wheel would've collapsed. And to make it worse he told me the horrid story of Mrs Piercey's daughter last week going down Shipton hill, whose wheel came off...

January 19, 1944

I hadn't scraped the mud off my shoes at 11 am on Monday before Miss Thomson suggested turning out the Morning Room, so there was no time for peak and pine. I found Mrs Thomson gently fading from life, a curious shadow of the Mrs Thomson who had me turning and burrowing out cupboards ten minutes after I arrived a year ago last August; it's sad for me, but I don't think it is for her. And I found Nurse Cavell who came to nurse the whoopers... She is cross eyed which makes her sound like a ventriloquist and she talks incessantly about the aristocracy she has nursed and she has a large draw-back of a black dog called Sally, who leaps up and knocks you down as soon as look at you. Yesterday, Tuesday, Miss Thomson went down to Minehead for a week, John Lovell went to Charlbury, David Lovell went somewhere else and Nurse Cavell went to bed with Migraine and I had to look after her *and* her dog, in case she has Something and gave it to Mrs Thomson... I found that she sleeps with her glasses on.

But I've been so beset with excitements – when I arrived I found a large parcel from Canada of what they call cast off clothes, but was really a partly worn rose tweed skirt and pale blue skirt and royal blue jumper and rose pink jumper and white satin petticoat and three bars of chocolate... I look simply wonderful in the royal blue jumper, a little less wonderful in the rose, and exceedingly doubtful in the rose skirt and pale blue. My plumpish hips have felt unobtrusive for so long in dunnish tweeds and blacks that I flinch at giving them so much pastel publicity. But perhaps in the spring.

Cotter's Bow,
January 27, 1944

This is the middle of the afternoon and I have snuck away to write to you and nothing has yet struck me dead. Such warm wind that I have all my window open and the children are calling and playing outside, the sun is shining and we have large patches of celandines under the trees. Might this be the spring of the peace year – it feels as if it might be.

Term is term again now, and we all started pleasantly for the first few days; school life has a great advantage because you can start again freshly and all forgotten three times a year . . . This term we have a nurse who is calm and capable of nursing the whole of Eton singlehanded – and has, if you believe all she says . . . But Nurse is a great pleasure to us: I've told you her eyes are this way and that; she never smiles but makes coy little heavy jokes with a solemn face. She was rather quiet for a day or so, but after she heard Mary Charles telling one of her outrageously dirty stories during supper washing up, she thinks she has gauged the tone of the whole staff and she whispers me into a corner and says: Did I ever tell you the One about the Utility chamber pots? Well, they have a rim and a handle and you put your own bottom in. But she never smiles.

January 31, 1944

Well, well, our Nurse Cavell is a one! To enforce her 'position' as she calls it, she turned out the other day with a bosom full of medal ribbons – this funny little water hen of a woman, and it turns out she nursed all through the last war in France and Gallipoli and finished up in charge of all the nursing Wrens and went to Lords on Army and Navy day with two admirals and a captain. That's as may be, but what really astounded me was that she nursed through two years in Spain in charge of a gang of nurses and equipment who offered themselves, half the gang and equipment to Franco and the other half to the government (Franco kept the equipment but refused the nurses, so they all nursed for the Government side)... She has a nice story about how she went for a trip to Germany without a word of German and the only way she could think of asking the policeman where the church was on Sunday was to go down on her knees and pray to him in the road, while a crowd gathered to watch her. As she said: You may think I'm a shy little mouse in England, but once you get me abroad I'm quite different: I sing in the street, I dance, and the red blood courses through my veins.

February 3, 1944

Congratulate me – I'm a member of the Women's Institute of Burford, and any minute now I shall be turning your velvet smoking jacket into a Settee for Two. It came about in a strange way: when... I went to the Boulters last Sunday night, Mrs Boulter talking of this and that asked me if I'd like to be a member of the W.I. I said hor hor laughing gaily and thinking that the sooner we got that out of our systems the better we should be and nothing more was said. Yesterday I went for my German lesson to Mr B, and he handed me a programme and said "This is the first Wednesday in the month and my wife has gone to the W.I. to propose you – will you look in under the Wesleyan Chapel on your way home and meet the President." – I learn a number of things but only a modicum of German... but it's worth it, because Ben is a thorough and charming and rambling scholar. However, we'd thoroughly dealt with pacifism and militarism by 5 to 4, and I thought it was time for me to skip the W.I. and rush home. But my conscience told me to be polite, and I dived under the Wesleyan and saw Mrs Boulter washing up. She hailed me as a new member, dried her hands on her apron, and introduced me to the President; then she handed me a stale bun and I helped her to dry up. And that was that. On March 1st is CEYLON by Georgina Battiscombe with eggs for the hospital.

Nurse Cavell is like a bran tub and every day I fish up another prize: last night she told me how she was a gold medal diplomatist in cooking from the Regent Street Polytechnic (probably one of her medal ribbons). One night the class was watching the chef from the Cecil make a cake and "he dipped his hand first in one pot and then in another saying Now you add this much of this and a pinch of that and stir in a bit of this... But I said Look here, I'm paying a guinea a lesson to watch you do this and you'd better measure it out in spoons so that I know where I am. And he looked at me as old fashioned as you like. But when the class was over he took me on one side and said If you want your omelettes to stay up, stir in a pinch of cornflour – and he never told that to anyone else."

February 5, 1944

Yesterday was Friday but I couldn't take my day out because of shortage of staff here and everyone too singlehanded to get the supper. I went to a café to tea and then chatted to Miss Bowerman who with everyone else is shuddering with horror at the batch of Americans in Burford. What silly fellows they are, and what unforeseeable damage our dislike of them will cause. I always feel a bit responsible for Americans and defend them – but these seem so consciously offensive. Mary Gardiner and I had an unpleasant time with a couple of semi drunks when we came back from the Boulters on Sunday night; Miss Bowerman has had small valuable things stolen from her shop, and Mrs North Lewis who keeps the Lamb, which is really slap-up and with a great number of valuable antiques in it, has had every portable piece of old china, pewter and copper stolen from her bar and lounge; and so it all goes, and resentment increases on both sides. Mr Griffen from the White Horse has written to the American C.O. to say he will have black Americans in his bar, but no whites. Also an American dropped a lighted match into the petrol hole of a civilian lorry while it was being filled in the High Street, and burnt the whole thing up, with fire engines in attendance. They are as good as a curfew because everyone is afraid of them at night, and Mary Gardiner and I will have to be very brave to go again to the Boulters tomorrow night.

February 10, 1944

Will you consider the possibility of my having my bun cut off when I have my next permanent wave and let me have your reaction as they say? I feel that in the Spring I might want to toss my head in Youthified and delicious freedom, but I'm also attached to my bun as a symbol of my five years dogged consistency.

February 16, 1944

. . . I laughed and laughed at my Valentine, and Miss Thomson took in the post so that she no doubt saw it too; she'll probably give me a little talk on pornographic postcards coming uncovered through the mail. I remember well that night I leaned out of the window clad only in my black tulle peignoir over my white serge camisole, and twisting my neck ever so slightly, saw Maudie Gumbold, brazen as brass, in your arms on the balcony above. I laughed rather bitterly to myself the next morning as I extracted rose thorns from your left ear when you told me you got them through bumping into the brass knob of the bed post, but from that day to this you never knew I knew . . .

February 19, 1944

. . . I went down to the Boulters where in an unguarded moment I'd offered to do some darning because Mrs B's eyes are bad, and I sat in the icy dining room trying to turn a sheet sides to middle with a machine that was so perverted that it golloped the cotton up in part of its entrails and then spewed it out in a sort of snowball of french knots every two minutes, and nothing I could do would make it any better. So Mrs Boulter went out to tea and I washed my hands of the machine and Ben and I had tea in front of the fire and he told me delightful tales of the days when he had a six room flat in Lincoln's Inn for £60 a year and went cycling all over France on nothing a week stopping at wayside inns where the wayside innmate was desole (accents intended) m'sieu, but all she could offer was soup, omelet, fried trout, cheese and coffee all for about 2½d as the franc was two a penny those days. Ah well. Then I came away, bearing one of Ben's shirts out of which he'd gouged a large hole and several rents; it all was so complicated that it had to be done in the solitude of my room.

I cycled over in drear cold not daring to hope that Mrs Stoter had made a fire, but she had, and she warmed and comforted me with a cup of Horlick's and told me she was counting the days till you came back. She gave me two slices of cold bacon and Mrs Crook gave me the largest egg I've ever seen with about three yolks in it, so I had all that for my supper and rode home by the light of my storm lantern swinging on my wrist. Snow was soft and thick on the road and the road was black and white striped where lorries have gone through.

February 22, 1944

I'd felt so sure that you would know when your leave was by now, that another letter with no date caught me unprepared for disappointment. Isn't it a sad thing that the only mental preparation one can make for living in these days is defence against disappointment or sadness or depression? I've forgotten what that other life was like when one took it as due that something good was just round the corner... Nothing here makes anything to write about. I've crossed Mrs Stoter's palm with silver to clean the cottage against your coming, and Tam with laudable gallantry has confessed to using a lavatory after they had all been told it was out of order, and jerking the handle which has split the china tank which I suppose I have to pay for, and will cost about £5 or £6. It must have been a stirring moment with the school in serried ranks and Miss Thomson saying: Now, I shan't punish any of you; one of you has broken the lavatory and your Mummy must pay for it. And Tam upping gaily and saying he did it. When he came to tell me about it he didn't seem to be at all sure exactly what was wrong and what he'd owned up to and what was broken, so that I can't be sure he wasn't slightly drunk with the nobility of sacrifice and limelight. I shall probably feel more deeply about it if Miss Thomson makes me pay.

Sunday March 12, 1944

What an amazing contrast to last Sunday's snow and cold with potatoes around the joint and slumber and toast for tea. There's a curious unnatural June warmth in the sun and the air seems to be rocking with the noise of birds... Tam is still in my room but it's only for another three weeks.* He keeps his atlas under his pillow and tosses it open as soon as I switch on the light at 6.45, before the sleep has cleared from his mind. I wish we could get hold of one of those cheap small globes so that I could assert with confidence that the earth is round and that the world is much larger than Switzerland even though the page is the same size.

* *There had been an outbreak of whooping cough in the school.* C.F.

March 19, 1944

... When I went to the Holloways for my milk on Friday the sun was as hot as summer on their yard and all the negroes-with-lorries were lying on their backs in the gravel doing nothing but just lie in the sun, and some were butting each other and running aimlessly after each other just like children, and they were laughing till their teeth were shining like Holloways' white pigeons. They are an admirable childlike people and enjoy what there is to be enjoyed with no restraint.

March 21, 1944
(the spring equinox, by golly)

... And wonderful beyond realizing is your news about 200 pounds a year from Jack Fry; the trouble is that I *don't* realize it. I tried pinching myself the way they do in books to keep themselves awake, and it didn't feel a bit like me pinching a rich woman... Monday morning was a fatal dank sort of morning and we were having breakfast dolefully in the stone barn they call the staff room and Pat was saying what she wanted to do when she grew up; I said that what I wanted right now was Riches, filthy blatant vulgar money with ivory telephones and peach crêpe-de-chine sheets and me with peroxided curls in a nightdress of pink ostrich feather tips receiving countless lovers who were all grey at the temples and distinguished and world weary – then the post came and there it all was except the ivory telephone. And I couldn't tell anyone... Do you remember those harassed days at the Mill when we used to think of the people who would never miss 200 pounds a year and what it would mean to us? You must teach me to be wise with it so that I don't expect it to go once round a mink coat and twice round a Sheraton tallboy...

... Last Sunday evening after tea I walked with Mary up into part of the Wychwood forest; the sun made a lemon horizontal light through the trees, and the small bushes were slightly spangled with green shoots and there were primroses and violets and anemones. Next June you must come with me to these woods.

Our Betty's boy friend Charlie told her that when he came back from Egypt there were about 40 girls on the boat being sent back because they were in Trouble. He said they all did it to get out of the army. It's a comforting thought that women can break away from all regimentation by the oldest most personal and unassailable reason. Charlie also said that the men on the boat were so disgusted that they didn't even speak to the girls, and that's a neat side-light on a man's view of morality.

March 27, 1944

What weather this is – sun as blazing as June for three days and a new moon as insubstantial as cigarette smoke; all the children having meals out of doors and Tam with his nose as freckled as a thrush's breast.

April 18, 1944

[After a bus ride to Wolvercote we] then went into Worcester College gardens which were bright and lovely. Tam took off his sandals and ran in the new grass and talked a long time to the swans and ducks; then we lay on the grass and 2 ducks and a drake miraculously came and squatted down at our feet, tucked their beaks into the backs of their wings, drew up their cream suede eyelids and went to sleep firmly enough for Tam to crawl up on his stomach and stroke their feathers.

April 25, 1944

. . . In the village on Mr Franklin's old empty shop is suddenly a large painted board: NO PROFANITY. Should you think the soldiers used to congregate there and all say DAMN at once? Margie Ward's solution is that No Profanity is probably American for Don't make a public convenience of yourselves just here.

Tam and I took the wheelbarrow along to the end of the road to collect John Lovell at 12.30 this morning in hot sun and piercing wind. While we were sitting on the grass 2 American airplanes dropped out of the sky on top of us; I thought they were crashing. Tam & I were flat on our faces quite instinctively to avoid being hit; I lifted my head and saw the grain of the wood under the paint as they grazed the branches on the hedge and swooped up.

May 3, 1944

Cotter's Bow again, and the sun shining on corridors of new yellow paint so that we walk bathed in sunshine, a new window knocked into the playroom wall so that more light and yet more light can get in; the apple trees are in bloom and the lilac and all of us are flowering and shining with the sun of new-termly endeavour – and no one has spoken a word above a gentle friendly voice. Tam is at the end of his book 3 in reading and has started a new exercise book for sums which will be a model of correctness. O all is so well with us – and what could be nicer than the beginning of a new term. Only, Miss Thomson and I, making her bed, look round the world and find the prospect is chaos and dismay, and I agree with you that for us looking at the deaths of Bob Kelly* and his like, Bob and his like are well out of it, except that each one of them is one who might have lifted the gloom a fraction into daylight.

* *Bob Kelly, who had been a pupil under my brother at Dunstable Grammar School, was a rear gunner in the Air Force, aged about nineteen. He wrote me many letters, between bombing raids on Germany, enclosing poems that he was writing.* C.F.

May 16, 1944

. . . I can't seem to get happy relations with any book since I left my Trollope behind me; I try and *try* with *Crime and Punishment*, but it's so painful it's like deliberately lowering yourself down into a long dark tunnel . . . It's like when I was a child and Mudge had shut me up in the darkish small boxroom without a window that we had at Cleeve Hill, and the only book in there was *Pilgrim's Progress* with slightly tinted horrifying Doré illustrations; I couldn't quite leave it alone but I got nothing but misery and fright from it.

The two Marys and I went down to the Boulters on Sunday night and found Mrs B just about to rush out after a frantic call from the Canteen to come and wash up the Sunday rush, so we went too, and I spent two solid hours breaking my back over sandwiches made with crumbly bread and hard margarine for gallant Americans. All the Americans seemed famished and grabbed a dozen sandwiches costing 2d each and I was left with empty plates to start again. My feet were killing me and I had blisters on my fingers, but as Mrs Boulter said: It brings the war home to you, doesn't it. And funnily enough I don't think she was joking.

May 20, 1944

. . . Mrs Stoter makes lumps come into my throat when she says: The irises were out last year when Mr Fry came on leave; we must get him back for the peas and new potatoes. I got up to the cottage expecting Mrs Stoter to have the boiler on so that we could have a bout of redying those green chair covers, but no boiler was on because she couldn't buy any dyes and not for want of trying. So it was all a relief, and as a thank-offering I turned out the cupboard under the stairs to get at your trunk, which had your school blazer vaguely perforated with moths, but nothing serious, and the wedding trousers, nothing perforated. So that's a relief. You've got to admire the ingenuity of a moth, getting into that closed trunk. Then without drawing a breath I rushed upstairs for a job I've always wanted to do – take up that dusty green carpet in our room and stain the floor. But it was more than I'd expected in the way of bed hoisting and carpet folding and lifting. I put it in the darkest part of the cupboard until we both feel strong enough to beat it some sunny day and it was an enormous relief to find Mrs S had borrowed my staining brush and couldn't find it. It was a good afternoon's work.

Such a funny thing: I wear gloves to sleep in after creaming my hands because they're getting so grimed and chapped – *Woman and Beauty* says so. The most suitable gloves I have are chamois leather and rather warm and always when I wake up in the morning I'm bare handed and my gloves are rolled neatly together under my pillow without disturbing me. It's fascinating to think of my subconscious doing all that by itself; I should like to be on more intimate terms with my subconscious anyway.

May 24, 1944

. . . I met a delightful person at the Boulters last Sunday: a thin-haired thin and unnoticeable young man with pencils clipped into his breast pocket, whose name is Dyer and who teaches Music and French at the Grammar School in Burford. He has a deformed right hand and arm and plays the piano brilliantly with it. By magic he extorts music of all sounds, qualities and instruments out of these country boys – if they won't play classical stuff he encourages syncopation. His method of keeping order by sheer force of a sort of innate involuntary authority is the wonder of the school porters so Mr Boulter tells me. I wish so much some of our staff could have heard him being surprised when Mary Charles suggested it was sometimes good that you should lose your temper with a child. His outlook as a teacher was completely satisfying to listen to, and I hear it all works brilliantly. The Headmaster says he's worth more salary than all the rest of his staff but he can't pay him more than 180 pounds a year because he hasn't a degree.

May 30, 1944

This is a bit too hot, don't you think? All our children are going around in nothing but shorts and bare backs, but they're too languid to play and the nights are agony when they all toss in a stew of churned sheets. There was a wonderful storm last evening with jags of electric blue lightning in the navy sky above the barn, the rain sizzled the ground but it's no cooler today. And today is Dancing with Miss Dancing Thomson, as white haired and pink faced and point device as a daisy and just as light on the stem.

June 7, 1944

. . . Monday was my German lesson, with me being really rather bright in a small way for the first time, and Ben Boulter falling into an endless anecdotage about the late Master of Balliol and Walter Pater, so that I thought I should be late for the only half hour I could spare to go and see an exhibition of one day only which had been whipped up at the last moment to fillip our Salute the Soldier week; an exhibition of old furniture, 14th and 15th (!) century paintings and engravings and objets d'art and books, at two houses opposite each other on Burford Hill.

Oh my darling, you should have been there. To think that these wonderful things are in houses in Burford being lived among . . . Breughel engravings, and Rembrandt etchings . . . There was a first edition of Blake's *Job* – 14th century German Bibles, a piece of 14th century Italian manuscript with colours fresh and lovely – oh misery to spend so little time among them. Then in the house over the way belonging to Mrs Something Cunningham there was furniture which made me weep with emotion . . . everything everything fine and rare and lovely and priceless. Over the fireplace was a metal crucifix of the 13th century . . . all ribs and muscles and anguish . . . Let's hurry and get passing rich so that I can do my darning wearing a carved jade thimble.

That was Monday. Tuesday was the invasion and my day out. The invasion news came at 1, and Miss Thomson immediately arranged Prayers for after dinner, and even after lentil soup and roly poly I was in such a state of emotion that I couldn't gulp O God Our Help. It was difficult to know exactly what to pray for, unless for the Allies to kill more people than the Germans. But it was a day fraught with awe.

June 28, 1944

Our sensation last week was an enormous Sherman tank in a vast convoy; the tank suddenly lost its caterpillar and crashed right over the side of our lovely Burford bridge, mercifully not quite killing five men inside and just missing several girls who had been standing in the little bays of the bridge. And there we were with every crane in the American army trying to get this monster out of the water and stones. The road was shut all Saturday while they worked and heaved, and by Sunday the foot traffic was going through Dr Cheatle's garden and over the bridge through the garden belonging to Mr Conway. And crowds gathered from all over the country, making a sort of Stow fair of it. For some reason when Miss Thomson took the school to church, it was forbidden to go through the gardens, so they appealed to Mr Conway's housekeeper, and with much raising of hats and wiping of boots the 25 children filed through a strange house and into church the back way, and were so excited to do the same thing going back, plus the sight of the cranes and the submerged tank, that no one concentrated on prayer. Finally by Sunday night they'd dragged the tank down the river and hauled it up on to Dr Cheatle's immaculate velvety lawn. But oh, our bridge.

The Buildings
July 29, 1944

Tam and I were driven up here by Mister yesterday after tea with a mountain of gipsy baggage: two years' accumulation of stuff and nonsense, and a new mop handle, and a hundred-year-old bee skip which Mr Crook gave as a parting gift, and a pot of strawberry jam, a pot of gooseberry jam, two pounds of honey, ½ lb of margarine, a pound of sultanas and a pound of sugar, as a parting gift from Mrs Crook. My parting gift from Mrs Thomson was the slightly frosty remark that she *had* hoped I would see them through the war, and from Miss Thomson a dazed damp hand and the assurance that 'right up to the end she hadn't believed I could do this to them.' Phew! I'm glad it's all over. Curious that I don't regret leaving them at all – probably just end of term weariness, and the pangs will come later if I'm lonely up here. There were always moments in the evening in Spring when the yellow rain-sun was on the grass and flowering apple trees and the children were playing in the garden, when I thought Miss Thomson had achieved the perfect unit of society: a strong house, 25 children, new grass, and flowering trees.

I'd asked Mrs Stoter vaguely in passing if she could sell me a few flowers to welcome ourselves home with but my goodness, every door and window was open showing vistas of flowers upstairs and downstairs in every receptacle and in the middle of the table a piece of resistance of her most precious crimson and lemon carnations mixed with what she calls a wisp of Gyps-Ophelia.

August 2, 1944

. . . Today has been the first bright sun and wind, and I washed my hair and streeled it in the heat like a free child of nature, all to save 5/-. In fact, it's rather disheartening to see what I look like when I do become a free child of nature – I shan't save many five shillingses this way, it's too disillusioning . . . Mrs Stoter has taken my bee skip and washed it thoroughly in the suds from her after-wash copper until it is bright gold. I was rather attached to some shreds of historic bee's wax and cells in it, but there were also even more historic dead bodies in it. It is looking most handsome as a workbasket standing by the side of John Keble's chair . . . It's a quarter to nine now . . . the sun is shining so brightly it looks as if it could never darken for night – have you seen this issue of the moon?

. . . Last evening I went to the Hewletts' to have a bath and coffee. I cycled back under a large very drowning moon which shone with a pearl colour on my bunch of white phlox in my bicycle basket and made them even more scented than in daytime. Ella wanted to know how I managed to fill in my time alone up here and why I didn't go down every evening. My goodness, life is such a whirl of jobs that I disorganised my entire routine to go down there for *one* night. Tam has to have his dinner at 12 these days because he is a farmer and harvesting in the mornings; in the afternoon we go down for the paper and shopping and sociability, and on the way back Tam stops at the New Road and cycles along to Churchill Piece where they are now cutting and binding. I come home, pack up his tea in a basket with a whisky bottle full of water, walk down the fields with it, walk back, have my tea, and walk down again to collect him from the tractor and drag him up the fields again, so tired he can hardly walk. Tonight he was clutching a khaki pheasant's egg which he expects me to blow tomorrow – heavens, how many years since I've blown a bird's egg? and it's bound to have a bird in it. Then bath and supper and part of the story and it's 7.30 and the tea things and bath things to be disposed of which makes it 8.15, then my two cups of coffee to be made and the evening's activities begin – and Ella wants to know what I do!

Tam and I are staining his floor and he's doing excellently. I needed great strength of mind to pass over to him the pot of stain and brush and leave him surrounded by cream skirting boards and pristine walls – but he has managed amazingly accurately and done practically the whole floor. He faltered at the end and contented himself by writing a large Tam Fry in stain on the cream boards which is supposed to stay there for ever and ever . . .

It may be the new strong summer heat or reaction from Cotter's Bow but I'm weighed upon by the most curious and heavy languor. I tell myself tut tut, but I'm swamped in it from the moment I get up until I go to bed. When I lift my fingers from the typewriter they weigh a ton and I hoist my head up with a wrench of mental strength. I'm so curious to know if I should sleep for 24 hours if I stopped struggling.

Tomorrow is Shipton flower show and Mrs Stoter is as busy as a bee. She hasn't really gone in for things like this before –

certainly not for prizes, but she feels that you must have a little public spirit in these days and it's not for the prize. Everything will be as excellent as all her doings are; she has prepared a tray covered in bright blue silk to exhibit her carrots on; her black flowered dress was washed today and blew on the line in the sun and wind, and I'm sure she and her exhibits will be the freshest and most savoury in the whole show. Tam somehow thinks his parsley and parsnips will have a s'prize; I opened my mouth to explain the system of entries and exhibits, but found myself suddenly overcome with excessive languor, so gave it up. I hope all passes off without rancour or misunderstanding.

August 6, 1944

Yesterday afternoon in blinding blazing sunshine was the flower show. Mrs Stoter had spent the morning in the dank oven of the YMCA hut arranging her produce – she returned exhausted and triumphant – first prize for her cottage garden, second for carnations and a bevy of 1sts 2nds and thirds for plates of gooseberries, potatoes, beetroots.

Tam and I went down about 2.30 and I spent the hottest afternoon I've ever spent on a hard bench in a rough tussocky field from 2.30 till 6 watching little boys and girls run 100 yards with a sweating vicar to start them off and two men in straw hats holding a piece of tangled string to stop them. Tam ran in everything of his age, coming in last and falling down with great joviality. But he came in *second* in one race and won 6d and he told the story to every stranger he met. Altogether the flower show was a great triumph for the Buildings.

Today is August Bank Holiday and Tam left me early to Holloway for the day and possibly the gymkhana at Chipping Norton. It was to have been my day of rest and relapse, but suddenly I've felt positively bouncing again and my lumbago has eased its deadly clench and I suddenly felt a large Monday wash was the thing to make me happy. I wondered if this should be my day for making acquaintance with the mystery of the copper, but it meant consultation with Mrs Stoter who is so harried with her evacuees Mrs Scholfield and daughter Reen and all the married daughters and husbands down for the weekend in navy trilbies and fancy waistcoats and pointed shoes who all turn up at meal times, that she's lost her good humour and has reached the sniff and head tossing stage of exasperation, and none of it seemed the time. But I washed and boiled in a saucepan and dishpan and hung out as snowy and professional wash as you'd ever see. I was so proud of it – I had to turn it to the sun and unpeg it and look at it and see if it was really as clean as it looked, then I took the wheelbarrow up to the wood for sticks so that I could see my washing tossing in the distance. I sat in a discreet place to brown my back where even the bullocks couldn't see me and thought of seagulls and clouds and other Georgian images to describe your pants on the line. It has been such a blazing day that even the pale brown cornfields are bleached of colour.

At 6 Mister brought Tam home covered in dust like a miller with flour and his hair mashed deep with gravel. He'd apparently spent the day at the farm gate dabbling in the dust the lorries flung over him. I washed his head under the wash house tap and streams of mud poured from his hair; while it was drying he rescued with exquisite care a moth that had fallen into the rain water tank and looked quite drowned; he eased it on to the grass to dry and it flapped its wings in the sun and flew away to Tam's joy. We have a strange and lovely moth that spent last night and today with us on our window sill – it is shaped exactly like a half ivy leaf, of the palest grape-green with a wine coloured line round the edge of its wings and a wine horizontal bar.

The Buildings
Saturday, August 12, 1944

. . . You will be edified to know that I found your son reading *Swann's Way* Part 1, and that he finds Proust a laughing matter: he was pealing with delicious laughter down here by the bookcase because he'd come upon the sentence in the first paragraph '. . . his thoughts ran into a channel . . .'. Tam repeated it over and over, completely overcome by the humour. This is all because Julia is quite a reader and has taken to the play of *Peter Pan* with prospect of all the other Barrie plays; I've finally settled Tam with *Wind in the Willows* and as I left him to see about Julia's bathing tonight, he was sitting up in bed with the book propped on his knees, looking unmistakeably Christopher Fry.

Julia is a nice child, and easy to cope with, she enjoys pottering far more than Tam and adopts a sophisticated matter; I was a bit startled yesterday when she said: "My *dear*, what *delicious* junket!" but I've forgotten what it feels like to be eleven.

After *all* my entreaties, they didn't send her bicycle, so going down the village is a bit complicated; we went down right after breakfast, Julia riding mine *down* while I walked and me riding back, which, with hills being higher than when I was a girl, means that I practically walk both ways – we must make other arrangements.

The Buildings
August 14, 1944

I'm completely dizzy with bewilderment; I don't know whether to let my bones dissolve in joy that you're coming home or whether to keep the upper lip still stiff in case – goodness knows what. So all my emotion is interior and the interior decorations are something lovely, my darling. (It's 10 o'c at night and I've just lit the lamp and I can't get it in the right place to light me).

My kettle is heating for my bath and that will be the end of this Monday that has gone on for so long that I don't remember Sunday at all. I got up at 6.30 this morning to do my washing before Mrs Stoter should be filling the wash house with tubs of blue water and heavings and wringings of serpentine sheets and clouds of steam and billowings of wood smoke. And Mrs Stoter, dear love, is tetchy to say the least these days – it's all the evacuees: Mrs Scholfield, she complains, looks so mournful and never takes her hair out of curlers and does her bits of washing in a basin and hangs them in her bedroom to dry, and that Reen – well, down she strolls at 10 looking as greasy as an old pork pie, slaps a bit of a damp flannel over her face and sits down with her feet up and her nose buried in a magazine, waiting for Mrs Stoter to give her breakfast; she never lifts a hand's turn to so much as do her shoes up yet she smells worse than Norrie after a day's harvesting. No wonder Mrs Stoter gets a bit vicious, yet her laugh is just as merry, and she went to immense pains to tell the grocer that now I was a customer I must be told when there were bits of suet, or it was custard week; she believes in fair do's all round. Then after breakfast I tore back to tidy the house and cook the dinner; then after dinner I got my children into their social clothes, took them to Ella's, gave them both a bath and took them to the Scotts for tea. I was bewildered with so many children and blazing sun, but Dr Scott showed me an exquisite, a perfect and unspeakably lovely painted Bohemian glass dessert service which you must see to believe. Also he has had a portrait of himself painted by Herbert Walker (the Tate Gallery do-er up of pictures) which I think is unspeakably bad; Dr Scott with a cream blancmange face in a porridge tussore suit . . . Then back to Ella's for three pounds of plums, our damp bath towels, and a lovely posy of flowers arranged for me in a bowl by Hazel – we had to bring bowl and all. Then up in blazing heat with Tam stopping at every cottage for drinks of water like an old man stopping at every pub, and to the gardener-with-the-dirty-mother for my Monday bunch of flowers, which were lovely this week – zinnias and dahlias and snapdragons, all in the red vase and making such a concatenation of red that it heats me to look at it. Then wash the children all over, all over again because they were dirty all over again, then suppers – then I begin to get a bit muzzy, because the jobs dwindled, but the sun still brilliant yellow at 9.30 and the men only just finishing harvesting for the day; never such harvest weather – Norrie and Carter *asked* if they could work on Sunday, they're so anxious to get it in.

O dearest and darling, what days – and you will soon be with me. Julia loves looking at those large Doré illustrated Infernos. I found her and Tam on their stomachs fascinated at the print of muscular men holding their heads and with their legs chopped off at the hips; Julia says there's one like that in Oxford, he plays the banjo.

[I went to direct *The School for Scandal* at the Theatre Royal, Bristol, in June 1945. *C.F.*]

June 26, 1945

Tam's new bicycle arrived – terrifyingly large, but it carried him there and back to Lyneham while I was wondering if his feet would reach the pedals. It has a pouch on the back with spanner and crowbar, and the whole prospect ahead is *horrifying* – the weekends will be nightmare and I expect he'll turn up in Bristol. This afternoon I made a skirt out of three old summer frocks – too too dirndl. The waist is teeny wee (my size) and it's so wide round the hem that we've used it to cover the new hayrick.

June 27, 1945

Has it sodden down with rain all day at Bristol, too? There has been no let or hindrance to the gloom; Norrie has stood in doorways shooting rusty cans and Mr Stoter spent a gloomy morning hammering a nail onto a hoe-handle, and the hens drooped their dripping feathers into the mud. I wore my new dirndl skirt to cheer me and I'm reading Byron's letters – what a *nice* man he was. How could he have come to be so misinterpreted by posterity, or at least, only half interpreted. I suppose the Byronic-philanderer element made for easy publicity – I must look out the Byron in Venice articles in *Horizon*. I might even read some of his poetry.

Tam is at home this evening for the first time since his bicycle arrived – he's doing some complicated landscape gardening in the pouring rain with 4 worn-out rubber tyres. – No, he has come in, with a hole *right* through the seat of his school trousers from riding on Norrie's tractor seat in the garage; like a lamb, and conscious of great guilt, he has sat down and written an excellent letter to Canada Granny (oh those thank you letters) complete with map from here to Lyneham and a picture of one of Mrs Avery's fried chips because he cycled down last night and stood in a queue for an hour for a shillingsworth of chips, and a horrider mess of limp pallid tepid grease and newspaper and potato you never saw. He loved it.

And now it's 9p.m. and he's bedded with a chapter of *Treas. Is.* and I'm sitting with my cup of coffee on the left hand and a pan of black currant jam brewing on the oil stove on my right. And you won't be able to eat any of it, you lucky fellow... Shepherd Faulkner's black currant bushes are swathed against the birds with mauve and grey chiffon which from a distance makes them look like Eliot's Eumenides. My black currant jam has a faint, a very faint, taste of cauliflower. How chic.

Bare Trees Against the Sky

for Phyl's Christmas Card 1985

You see how these trees are showing
   The days and years of reaching out to the light –
All the more clearly because the leaves
   By falling have made the complexity
         Into a kind of music –

And how love, too, over the days and years
   Has drawn a clear pattern of living tracery
Against our winter sky, and the sky
         Has no boundaries.

C.F.